P9-DJA-182

GRACES

GRACES

Prayers and Poems for Everyday Meals and Special Occasions

June Cotner

HarperSanFrancisco
A Division of HarperCollins*Publishers*

 For information address HarperCollins Publishers, 10 East 53rd Street, New York, NY 10022.

Permission and acknowledgments begin on page 185.
Book design and illustration by Laurie Anderson.

Library of Congress Cataloging-in-Publication Data:
Cotner, June.
Graces : prayers and poems for everyday meals and special occasions / June Cotner. — 1st ed.
p. cm.
ISBN 0–06–065956–4 (cloth : alk. paper).
ISBN 0–06–065957–2 (pbk. : alk. paper)
1. Prayers. 2. Devotional literature. 3. Grace at meals. I. Title.
BL560.C68 1994
291.4'3—dc20 94–8034
CIP

---

94 95 96 97 98 ❖ HAD 10 9 8 7 6 5 4 3

This edition is printed on acid-free paper that meets the American National Standards Institute Z39.48 Standard.

This book is dedicated with love and appreciation to Steve, Kyle, and Kirsten. Thanks for the countless hours you each spent with attentive ears to help me pick my way through hundreds of possible poems and prayers for the book.

CONTENTS

2 Seasonal Graces

3 For Holidays

4 For Family Gatherings

10 Short Graces

11 From Around the World

12 For Peace and Justice

13 For Contemplation

THANKS

I owe much gratitude to both my agent, Denise Marcil, and my editor, Barbara Moulton, for their shared vision of the possibilities of a book like *Graces.* I received many submissions from around the country, and both Denise and Barbara liked the idea that a number of friends, families, and poets (of all ages and religious beliefs) would critique the manuscript and help select the content of the final version.

I'd especially like to thank the following friends, relatives, and professional acquaintances who critiqued the manuscript: Arnie Anfinson, James Bertolino, James Broughton, Patty Cheng, Susan Gerrish, Fern Halgren, Seth Hartmann, Denise Marcil, Barbara Moulton, Kirsten Myrvang, Kyle Myrvang, Steve Myrvang, and Ron Sharp.

Special thanks go to Joan Almon of the Waldorf Kindergarten Association for submitting children's graces, to Sue

Gitch for help in finding music and lyrics for the musical graces, to Joyce Standish for her independent editing assistance, to Marion Swanson for her secretarial and emotional support throughout the project, and to *Writer's Digest* for listing a call for submissions.

The deepest appreciation is due to the contributors themselves. Your ways of expressing your connection and gratitude to God or a higher spiritual power (however you may define him or her) emanate from these pages.

INTRODUCTION

Graces began as a notebook collection that I had compiled to enhance and celebrate our family's mealtime gatherings. It evolved out of a desire to bring something more interesting to the dinner table than uninspired graces memorized by rote. How many families face the same dilemma? The perennial question, "Who wants to say grace?" is often met with a slight feeling of dread rather than joy. When the same graces are repeated again and again, praying becomes mechanical instead of providing a passionate connection with life and a higher spiritual power. On a trip west, my agent, Denise Marcil, looked at my *Graces* collection and felt it would have widespread appeal. She presented the manuscript to Barbara Moulton, senior editor at Harper San Francisco, who felt it would make a perfect book for her publishing house. Both Denise and Barbara thought the book would be strengthened by including original, previously unpublished, submissions. I put an announcement in *Writer's Digest* and soon my mailbox was filled with inspiring poems and prayers from all over the country. My task became that of a gardener as I picked my bouquet from so beautiful a garden. I heard from (and included several poems by) two people in their nineties (Ruth Rose and Thomas Elwood).

Graces is significantly different from any other book of graces or prayers. The content reflects the evolving need for fresher spiritual offerings. In an attempt to create an original, nontraditional grace book, some of the graces, such as "Lilacs," should be looked upon as meditations on the beauty of life for which we express our gratitude to God. Wherever possible, I did my best to eliminate gender-specific references to God. For ease in using the book, the poems and prayers are organized around themes, an aid for those in search of a grace to fit a particular occasion.

I do hope that *Graces* will help families and individuals who are seeking new ways to feel strongly connected to each other and to a higher spiritual power. The ritual of a mealtime grace can provide us with a crucial sense of personal and spiritual identity as well as the opportunity to express gratitude for feeling bonded by our common humanity.

If you have a poem or prayer to submit for a future book of graces, please send it to:

June Cotner
P.O. Box 2765
Poulsbo, WA 98370

All submissions should be typed, double-spaced, and should include your name, address, and phone number at the top of each page; those accompanied by a self-addressed, stamped envelope will eventually receive a reply.

I

For Any Gathering

MORNING GRACE

We thank Thee God
as we watch
the distant hills
suddenly emerge
above the filmy, white mist
and gently touch heaven—
awakening the sun
for another day.

JOAN STEPHEN

SANSKRIT SALUTATION TO THE DAWN

Listen to the salutation to the dawn,
Look to this day for it is life, the very life of life,
In its brief course lie all the verities and realities of our existence.

The bliss of growth, the splendour of beauty,
For yesterday is but a dream and tomorrow is only a vision,
But today well spent makes every yesterday a dream of happiness
and every tomorrow a vision of hope.
Look well therefore to this day.
Such is the salutation to the dawn.

AUTHOR UNKNOWN

GRACE AT BREAKFAST

O Lord, as now we break the fast
We thank Thee for the night safe passed.
Now grant safekeeping on our way,
Good cheer and strength and health all day.

THOMAS ELWOOD

BLESSED BE

All life is your own,
All fruits of the earth
Are fruits of your womb,
Your union, your dance.
Lady and Lord,
We thank you for blessings and abundance.
Join with us, Feast with us, Enjoy with us!
Blessed be.

STARHAWK

GRACE FOR DIETING

Are there graces for lettuce, Lord? And low-fat, no-fat, meat-free, fun-free meals? I need you to send me words for blessing this paltry meal before me, Lord, for it is difficult to feel grateful for these skimpy portions when all I think of are the foods *not* on my plate. Help me change that thought, to make peace with choosing not to eat them, for I need help in becoming the healthier person I want to be. Hold up for me a mirror of the new creation you see me to be, for I need a companion at this table, Lord.

MARGARET ANNE HUFFMAN

AN EARLY SAINT'S PRAYER

Give us, O Lord, thankful
hearts which never forget
Your goodness to us.
Give us, O Lord, grateful
hearts, which do not waste
time complaining.

SAINT THOMAS AQUINAS
(1225–1274)

OUR PURPOSE IN LIFE

Dear God, at some time, we each ask ourselves what our place or purpose is in life. We wonder what difference it makes that we exist, what our role is in the larger scheme of things. We question whether it's worth the trouble to work hard at our lives, to learn all we can, to grow into the best person we can possibly be. The contribution we made compared to all our efforts may seem very small.

But all large, important things are made up of many small, seemingly insignificant parts. Every person is part of the world, of human history, of the energy of the planet and the universe. Amen.

VERONICA RAY

PRAYER FOR OUR HOME

God of mercy,
God of grace,
Be pleased to bless
This dwelling place.
May peace and kindly deeds
Be found;
May gratitude and love
Abound.

NORMA WOODBRIDGE

FAMILY PRAYER

Lord, behold our family here assembled.
We thank you for this place in which we dwell,
for the love that unites us,
for the peace accorded us this day,
for the hope with which we expect the morrow;
for the health, the work, the food and the bright skies
that make our lives delightful;
for our friends in all parts of the earth. Amen.

ROBERT LOUIS STEVENSON
(1850–1894)

A HYLANDER'S BLESSING

May your heart stay as active
and young as your mind.

May your kindnesses to others
be returned ten-fold, in kind.

May life's adversities be
light, and easy to bear.

May joy and peace quickly
dry up each tiny tear.

May you always be able
to count on one good friend.

May God's Grace light up
your road, to its very end.

THOMAS K. HYLAND, JR.

THE 23RD PSALM REVISITED

The Lord is my Shepherd
We've had a great time
He's helped me to see the green pastures
Not just with my eyes, but with my heart
And to love the life there
And everywhere.
He was quiet with me beside
Still waters
That quenched the thirst
Of my soul.
He let me fall and fall again
Until I knew that my only happiness
was through learning
to Love like He does.
Some of us fear what they call death,
But the secret of Eternity
Is that it's all Life and Love,
And Heaven is a feast of Joy,
For nothing else exists
But the All that is God.
So I sing the song of the Universe
That we all know
In the part of us
That is Forever.

KATIE GOODE

WE CLOSE OUR EYES

We close our eyes,
we bow our heads
and offer thanks
for daily bread.

For friends and family
gathered near
for forests and rivers
for elk and deer.

For oceans and mountains
for plant and stone
for all that we feel
for love, beauty and home.

And when the day comes
that we must say good-bye,
we thank you, dear God,
for the tears we shall cry.

And our children shall sit
with their own children small,
and give thanks, once again,
for the miracle of it all.

STEVE MYRVANG

MOUNTAIN LULLABY

May your sleep find
the angel of four wishes,
and your fists unfold
to blossoms of pink.

May your fears lapse
like fallen leaves, and may wind
in the bare trees
purify your breathing.

May moonlight on the mountains
bring a song of gathering,
and Gaia enter your dreams
to teach you symbiosis

the way your first lover
taught you to kiss.

JAMES BERTOLINO

A GROUP GRACE

Let's join hands in a circle, please.

Now look around the circle, recognizing and acknowledging each of God's beautiful creations with us this day.

Let's close our eyes for a moment and think back over the day just past, the good parts of the day, and the not so good parts. (pause)

And now, take a deep breath and become aware of the godliness which you and each one of us expresses in our lives.

We thank God for that awareness of that love and power at work in our lives. We accept it in love. We bless this food of which we are about to partake, and the loving souls which have prepared it. For this world, this love and this awareness, we say, "Thank you, Father-Mother God." Amen.

THE REVEREND BOB BIDDICK

I THANK THEE

For diamond-studded velvet
  Behind a silver moon
For music of the nightwinds,
  A nightingale's sweet tune—
    For whispering trees
    And darkening peace—
  I Thank Thee.

For mountains carved of sea pearls
  For clouds that shroud their heights
For pristine air like nectar
  And ghostly northern lights
    For misty vales
    And secret dales—
  I Thank Thee.

For fiery fuchsia ribbons
  That stream across the sky
For opalescent sunsets
  And mornings dipped in dye
    For mornings pale
    And day's finale—
  I Thank Thee.

For scents that herald springtime
For lilac-haunted nooks
For violet's purple fragrance
And merry, trickling brooks—
For little things
That give souls wings—
I Thank Thee.

MONICA MILLER

CELEBRATION

May peace enter the hearts
  of all who join with us
  and share the joy of this day.

For the treasured friendship
  of those gathered here,
We ask your blessing, Lord.

For the special gift
  of love we share,
We ask your blessing, Lord.

For the oneness of heart
  that brings us together,
We ask your blessing, Lord.

For those whose lives
  we will touch today,
We ask your blessing, Lord.

For those who have prepared this meal
  and the food we are about to enjoy,
We ask your blessing, Lord.

THERESA MARY GRASS

BLESSING

In the name of the Father,
 whose love sustains us,
And of the Son,
 whose life regains us,
And of the Holy Spirit,
 whose guidance maintains us,
We ask a blessing on this meal.

THERESA MARY GRASS

2

Seasonal Graces

PSALM OF PRAISE

Sing for joy in summer
When earth is bright and green.
Sing with fun in winter
When snow is velveteen.
In spring sing out with gusto
For the life to soon unfold—
And sing with zest in autumn
For the woodlands colored gold.

JOAN STEPHEN

SPRING

We give you everlasting thanks, O God,
For the marvels of your great creation.

As the flowers blossom and bloom around us
We lift our hearts in joy and celebration.
Amen.

JOYCE BLAKNEY DUERR

A SPRING CROCUS:
For the Children of AIDS

There are children
who diminish
as they grow,

who will never be grown,
or be parents,
or be old.

Their few days smolder
like the sun rising
into a storm.

And those who love
hold them precious
and brave

as the first Spring crocus,
whose small yellow blaze
might brighten

a morning still held dim
by Winter. Such
blossoming

refutes the cold.

JAMES BERTOLINO

LILACS

I'm
seldom stunned

But this morning
the dewborne scent
of fresh morning lilacs
sent me staggering in a daze

Indeed,
it was a shock
of windblown power
so fragrant, so potent

It leveled me
with a sweet purple jolt

GARY E. MCCORMICK

SUMMER

We welcome summer and the glorious blessing of light. We are rich with light; we are loved by the sun. Let us empty our hearts into the brilliance. Let us pour our darkness into the glorious, forgiving light. For this loving abundance let us give thanks and offer our joy.
Amen.

MICHAEL LEUNIG

A SUMMER GRACE

We thank You for white daisies
that float on slender stems
above the golden grass,
star the summer field
with dazzling little poems
from the universe
and will not let me pass.

THELMA J. PALMER

THE ISLAND, THIS SEASON

The corn stalks are broken.
Potatoes are cached in dark corners,
onions and garlic braided
and hung. Gold peaches
in glass and plums'
rich ruby. Black pulp of berries
thickens in jars. Split cedar
is stacked by the door
and the lamps filled.

Anchored all night in the eyes
of this wind, the house
billows toward stars.

ALICIA HOKANSON

WINTER VISION

The fine snow falls
Like the last breath
Of a soft whisper
As it changes its name
On the lips of a slow stream.

It comes very quickly
This winter vision
In the wink of a swift instant
On this will-o'-the-wisp evening.

GARY E. MCCORMICK

DECEMBER BLESSING

One
silver
birdsong
rings
the Christmas meadow
and
blossoms
my heart
to a rose

THELMA J. PALMER

LITANY FOR LIGHT

Let us rejoice for Spring
and the return of luminous light;
the sweetness and glory
of blossom and bud,
fruit and foliage;
the balm of softer winds and restorative rain.
Let us give thanks for lengthening daylight
after months of shadows;
more light for the sprouting of seeds,
added light for emerging animals;
a purity of light to awaken the soul
to a shining re-dedication
to appreciate Earth's wondrous fragility.
Let us praise
the gift of each lustrous day
from dawn's rippling bird-choir ebullition
to twilight's blue silence of serenity.

SHEILA CONSTANCE FORSYTH

3

For Holidays

A GAELIC BLESSING FOR SAINT PATRICK'S DAY

May the road rise to meet you,
may the wind be always at your back,
may the sun shine warm on your face,
the rain fall softly on your fields;
and until we meet again,
may God hold you in the palm of his hand.

AUTHOR UNKNOWN

EASTER INVOCATION

What do I ask for in one word, one breath: Yourself, that's all and everything.

SHIRLEY ASANO GULDIMANN

EASTER SONG

God speaks in words of comfort, cheer,
The joys of early Spring,
The hyacinth and daffodil,
Hope that robins bring.
Blue speckled eggs in downy nest,
The crocus is in bloom.
All God's world, a garden fair,
And triumph o'er the tomb.

NORMA WOODBRIDGE

EASTER MEAL GRACE

We are celebrating today, Lord, a mixture of bunnies hiding colored eggs and angels rolling away stones. Join us as we gather to share a meal and ponder both, enjoying the one and giving thanks for the other. Bless those about this table savoring both the food and the message of this day. Remind us, too, Lord of unexpected appearances, that this also is the season of spring, a time when rebirth is not so surprising after all. Send us after lunch into the yard where, while hiding colored Easter eggs for the children, we may suddenly understand what this day really means.

MARGARET ANNE HUFFMAN

FOR MOTHER'S DAY

Dedicated to all mothers, everywhere; but especially those in heaven.

Who was it that bore us in the womb,
and carried such a treasure, day by day?
Was it you that took the pain and cried,
'til we saw the first break of day?

Who nursed us, bathed us, dressed us,
sang lullabies to ease life's pain,
and when we cried, tenderly caressed us,
'til peaceful slumber came again?

Who stitched and sewed, and ironed all night,
so we could proudly stroll to school?
And who also taught us wrong from right,
spared the rod, and used the "Golden Rule"?

Who scrubbed the floors, cooked our meals,
and labored hard each and every day,
just so we would know how it feels,
to enjoy our childhood's play?

Who sacrificed, and did without,
so we would know no shame,
and many times, took Father's clout,
when really, *we* were to blame?

As time went by, we spread our wings,
and oft' we were apt to go astray;
but, as we went out to "do our things,"
whose watchful eye was there to guide our way?

The years have flown swiftly by,
and time has made us much the wiser,
as now we raise our glasses high,
who here can not now praise *her?*

Thank you, Mother Dear—please hear us!

THOMAS K. HYLAND, JR.

MEMORIAL DAY PICNIC GRACE

Surrounded by a community of headstones, Lord, we both remember and mourn and celebrate and play, for this day reminds us that to have one, we have had the other. Thank you for our history written by those strangers fallen in battle to ensure our freedom-filled lives of safety. Thank you, too, for our own ancestors whose efforts still course through our lives in strengths, names, and accomplishments we pause to honor.

Now bless our picnics and parties as we join in the parade of those remembering, those remembered.

MARGARET ANNE HUFFMAN

FOR FATHER'S DAY

(Little Man)

Little Man how fast you grew
And went the way all children do
Into a world you've yet to know,
You needed room to stretch and grow.

I watched with pride as you felt your way
And tested strengths in work and play.
We shared our fun as buddies do—
When you were cut I bled some too.

Shooting the rapids or climbing high,
Gazing at stars in a western sky;
We gave it our best just like a team,
A young man's game—an old man's dream.

I'll always treasure those memories past,
Could prayers but make the good times last.
But boys were meant to grow up strong
And daddies can't just tag along.

So I hope you know and understand
I'm always near if you need a hand,
And of all God's gifts could I choose but one . . .
It would be a father's love for his son.

C. DAVID HAY

GRANDPARENTS' DAY

(This holiday is celebrated the second Sunday of September.)

They've added a new holiday, Lord, a day to honor the grandparents who tended us so well. Pause with us as we play again in the dusty lanes of childhood at Grandma and Grandpa's house; as we realize again that we are so special that you gave us these bigger-than-life companions to help bridge home and away, childhood and maturity. In their footsteps, we made the journey. Thank you for such a heritage.

MARGARET ANNE HUFFMAN

HALLOWEEN GRACE

Amidst hobgoblins and pranksters, Lord, we seek a quiet corner this autumn evening, to give thanks for the saints whose day this really is. Be tolerant of our commercialized, costumed fun, even as you remind us of the pillars of faith upon whose shoulders we stand today. Keep our trick-or-treating fun, clean, and safe, our faith memories aware, for it is too easy to lose track of what we really celebrate in the darkness of this night.

MARGARET ANNE HUFFMAN

THANKSGIVING DAY PRAYER

We take so much for granted
of life and liberty,
and think that we deserve it;
that all was done "for me."

Think how they must have struggled,
new pilgrims in this land.
So many died from hardships
yet still they made a stand.

When all the work was finished,
new crops sowed in the ground,
they gathered with their neighbors,
asked blessings all around.

Oh, God, help us be grateful
for gifts you've sent our way.
For these we want to thank you
on this Thanksgiving day.

KRIS EDIGER

THANKSGIVING BLESSINGS

Lord be with us on this day of thanksgiving
Help us make the most of this life we are living
As we are about to partake of this bountiful meal
Let us not forget the needy and the hunger they feel
Help us to show compassion in all that we do
And for all our many blessings we say thank you

HELEN LATHAM

THANKSGIVING GRACE

(All join hands around the table.)

This is a day for *thanks.*
A day in which we
see or hear or feel
the wonders of the other
moments of the year.
This is a day for *time.*
A day in which we
think of pasts that make
our present rich
and future bountiful.
This is a day for *joy.*
A day in which we share a gift of laughter
warm and gentle
as a smile.
Above all, this is a day for *peace.*
So let us
touch each other
and know that
we are one.
For these and other blessings,
we thank Thee, God.

DANIEL ROSELLE

ADVENT

Into the bleakest winters of our souls, Lord, you are tip-toeing on tiny Infant feet to find us, hold our hands. May we drop whatever it is we are so busy about these days to accept this gesture so small that it may get overlooked in our frantic search for something massive and overwhelming. Remind us that it is not you who demands large, lavish celebrations and enormous strobe-lit displays of faith. Rather, you ask only that we have the faith of a mustard seed and willingness to let a small hand take ours. We are ready.

MARGARET ANNE HUFFMAN

CHANUKAH MESSAGE

May God protect us from our foes,
Like candles from the past.
As Faith unites, and gives, and welds
The essence that will last.
To give and take,
And feel and love,
Is that which we must treasure.
The Faith in it shines brighter than
A mortal eye can measure.

JOSEPH L. BYRON

CHANUKAH LIGHTS

On eight nights,
we light candles.
We light them from memory,
Beginning with the first miracle
of Chanukah,
when a light burned
in the Holy Temple
for eight days and nights,
without any help
except faith.
And it was enough.

MARJORIE GAIL PEVNER

CHRISTMAS EVE DINNER

The Christmas tree, Lord, is groaning beneath gift-wrapped anticipation; the table before us is resplendent with shared foods prepared by loving hands for which we give thanks. And now, as this waiting season ticks to a bell-ringing, midnight-marvelous close, we gathered around this table are scooting over to make room for the anticipated Guest. Come join us, blessing us with the gift of your presence as we say, "Welcome."

MARGARET ANNE HUFFMAN

CREDO AT CHRISTMAS

At Christmas time I believe the things that children do.

I believe with English children that holly placed in windows will protect our homes from evil.

I believe with Swiss children that the touch of edelweiss will charm a person with love.

I believe with Italian children that La Befana is not an ugly doll but a good fairy who will gladden the hearts of all.

I believe with Greek children that coins concealed in freshly baked loaves of bread will bring good luck to anyone who finds them.

I believe with German children that the sight of a Christmas tree will lessen hostility among adults.

I believe with French children that lentils soaked and planted in a bowl will rekindle life in people who have lost hope.

I believe with Dutch children that the horse Sleipner will fly through the sky and fill the earth with joy.

I believe with Swedish children that Jultomte will come and deliver gifts to the poor as well as to the rich.

I believe with Finnish children that parties held on St. Stephen's Day will erase sorrow.

I believe with Danish children that the music of a band playing from a church tower will strengthen humankind.

I believe with Bulgarian children that sparks from a Christmas log will create warmth in human souls.
I believe with American children that the sending of Christmas cards will build friendships.
I believe with all children that there will be peace on earth.

DANIEL ROSELLE

CHRISTMAS COME

Day of light,
Day of birth,
Here is God
Come to earth.

JOANNA M. WESTON

CHRISTMAS PRAYER

May the spirit of giving,
Go on through the year,
Bringing love, laughter,
Hope, and good cheer.
Gifts wrapped with charity,
Joy, peace, and grace,
Ribboned with happiness,
A tender embrace.

NORMA WOODBRIDGE

A NEW YEAR'S EVE PRAYER

A new year is approaching;
What does it hold for me?
It may bring joy or sorrow;
Oh, God, what shall it be?

Sometimes my heart is anxious—
I think that I should know
The way into the future—
Each step that I will go.

But You, in Your great wisdom
Must plan for me my all
Lest as Your child I falter
And miss Your perfect call.

Dear Lord, I pray for guidance
In all I say and do,
And then the year upcoming
Will truly honor You!

MILDRED M. SMITH

A NEW YEAR

As the new year dawns upon us
We seek your forgiveness for the sins of the past.

May our one resolution for this coming year
Be to walk with you from the first day to the last.

Fill each day with a new awareness of your presence
And make us a blessing to those around us.

JOYCE BLAKNEY DUERR

4

For Family Gatherings

A WEDDING TOAST

May your love be firm,
and may your dream of life together
be a river between two shores—
by day bathed in sunlight, and by night
illuminated from within. May the heron
carry news of you to the heavens, and the salmon bring
the sea's blue grace. May your twin thoughts spiral upward
like leafy vines, like fiddle strings in the wind,
and be as noble as the Douglas fir.
May you never find yourselves back to back
without love pulling you around
into each other's arms.

JAMES BERTOLINO

THE EVE OF A WEDDING
(Love's Philosophy)

The fountains mingle with the river,
  And the rivers with the ocean;
The winds of heaven mix forever,
  With a sweet emotion;
Nothing in the world is single;
  All things by a law divine
In one another's being mingle:—
  Why not I with thine?

See! the mountains kiss high heaven,
  And the waves clasp one another;
No sister flower would be forgiven
  If it disdained its brother;
And the sunlight clasps the earth,
  And the moonbeams kiss the sea:—
What are all these kissings worth,
  If thou kiss not me?

PERCY BYSSHE SHELLEY
ENGLISH LYRIC POET (1792–1822)

WEDDING REHEARSAL DINNER GRACE

Welcome to our party, oh Lord of water-into-wine feastings. For poised at the edge of a great venture are these two people we each hold in our hearts as special. Be with them on this the final eve of their separateness, for soon they will become a union. Be present at their daily table as you are with them tonight. And be, Lord, with us, too, their friends and family, as we share a meal, a memory, a toast for new beginnings.

MARGARET ANNE HUFFMAN

THE WEDDING FEAST

(Love)

I love you,
Not only for what you are,
But for what I am
When I am with you.

I love you,
Not only for what
You have made of yourself,
But for what
You are making of me.

I love you
For the part of me
That you bring out;
I love you
For putting your hand
Into my heaped-up heart
And passing over
All the foolish, weak things
That you can't help
Dimly seeing there,
And for drawing out
Into the light

All the beautiful belongings
That no one else had looked
Quite far enough to find.

I love you because you
Are helping me to make
Of the lumber of my life
Not a tavern
But a temple;
Out of the works
Of my every day
Not a reproach
But a song.

I love you
Because you have done
More than any creed
Could have done
To make me good,
And more than any fate
Could have done
To make me happy.

You have done it
Without a touch,
Without a word,
Without a sign.
You have done it
By being yourself.
Perhaps that is what
Being a friend means,
After all.

ROY CROFT

FOR A WEDDING OR ANNIVERSARY
(I Want You)

I want you when the shades of eve are falling
  And purpling shadows drift across the land;
When sleepy birds to loving mates are calling—
  I want the soothing softness of your hand.

I want you when the stars shine up above me,
  And Heaven's flooded with the bright moonlight;
I want you with your arms and lips to love me
  Throughout the wonder watches of the night.

I want you when in dreams I still remember
  The ling'ring of your kiss—for old times' sake—
With all your gentle ways, so sweetly tender,
  I want you in the morning when I wake.

I want you when the day is at its noontime,
  Sun-steeped and quiet, or drenched with sheets of rain;
I want you when the roses bloom in June-time;
  I want you when the violets come again.

I want you when my soul is thrilled with passion;
  I want you when I'm weary and depressed;
I want you when in lazy, slumbrous fashion
  My senses need the haven of your breast.

I want you when through field and wood I'm roaming;
  I want you when I'm standing on the shore;
I want you when the summer birds are homing—
  And when they've flown—I want you more and more.

I want you, dear, through every changing season;
  I want you with a tear or with a smile;
I want you more than any rhyme or reason—
  I want you, want you, want you—all the while.

ARTHUR L. GILLOM

WEDDING ANNIVERSARY GRACE

There is no greater mystery, oh Lord of covenants and promises, than love. And so we surround these, our friends and kin, to honor their steadfast living within this mystery, within the fullness of married love, surely one of the greatest mysteries of all. Help them to honor their past even as they create a future, using the pleasures and applause of this present day, Lord, a time when we all kneel before their accomplishments, an inspiration to us all.

MARGARET ANNE HUFFMAN

AN ANNIVERSARY CELEBRATION

(We Have Lived and Loved Together) (adapted)

We have lived and loved together
  Through many changing years;
We have shared each other's gladness
  And wept each other's tears;
I have known ne'er a sorrow
  That was long unsoothed by thee;
For thy smiles can make a summer
  Where darkness else would be.

Like the leaves that fall around us
  In autumn's fading hours,
We both can speak of one love
  Which time can never change.

We have lived and loved together
  Through many changing years,
We have shared each other's gladness
  And wept each other's tears.
And let us hope the future,
  As the past has been will be:
I will share with thee thy sorrows,
  And thou thy joys with me.

CHARLES JEFFERYS

NEW BABY

The new baby, Lord, sits centerpiece proud on the dining table as we eat a sleepy, still incredulous meal. Where before there were only two at our table, now there is a family eating together. Only you, creator, could come up with such a marvel, and we are awed even in the midst of exhaustion and newness. May our family dinner conversations, like the meals ahead, nourish and fill as we continue the creating you have begun, the making of a family.

MARGARET ANNE HUFFMAN

MILESTONE BIRTHDAY GRACE

Join us at this candle-lit festival of birthday celebration, Lord, for this our special loved one. Join us as we laugh and joke about golden ages, silver hairs, for our laughter is bubbling up from gratitude that the years are only enriching this special celebrant. And, Lord, enriching our lives as friends and family as well, for we are the ones receiving the best birthday gift today: the gift of knowing this special person. Thank you for the gift.

MARGARET ANNE HUFFMAN

BIRTHDAYS

Your birthdays, dear, are like a harp
  Whose strings, like silken wings
  Bring memories of melodies—
  Of fond, familiar things.

May future joys like golden noise
  Resound throughout your days,
And health be strong and wealth be long
  And happiness always.

THOMAS ELWOOD

I WONDER IF GOD HAS A BIRTHDAY

I wonder if God has a birthday
a date to call his own
some time set aside in creation
the day to us unknown.

I wonder if he'd like big presents,
a cake with gooey trim.
Could all of the world join in singing
the "birthday song" to him?

I wonder if God blew out candles
would stars begin to fall?
And can't you imagine the angels
really having a ball?

I wonder if God has his birthday
established by the plan
to celebrate life's own beginning,
the day it all began.

I wonder if someday he'll tell us
when we see his face.
Do you think he'll throw a grand party
at his heavenly place?

I wonder if God has a birthday
A special day, it's true
some time set aside in creation
I wonder, haven't you?

KRIS EDIGER

FOR OUR CHILDREN

We give thanks for our children.
May we continue to be blessed
by their simple wonder
so that we might not take
for granted one single moment
of this miracle to which
we've been born.

STEVE MYRVANG

FOR A FAMILY REUNION

Lord bless this gathering of our family
We ask that our bond of love lasts eternally
Help us realize how much we mean to each other
This close-knit group of father, mother, sister, brother
Aunts, uncles, cousins, and many more
May they always feel welcome at our door
Look down on us Lord from above
And surround us all with thy divine love

HELEN LATHAM

NORTHWEST INDIAN MEMORIAL ON DEATH

Do not stand at my grave and weep.
I am not there.
I do not sleep.
I am a thousand winds that blow.
I am the diamond glint on snow.
I am the sunlight on ripened grain.
I am the autumn rain.
When you awake in the morning hush,
I am the swift uplifting rush
Of birds circling in flight.
I am the stars that shine at night.
Do not stand at my grave and weep.
I am not there.
I do not sleep.

AUTHOR UNKNOWN

THE CIRCLE OF LIFE

Fear not that which is now,
Fear not that which is to come.
Life, Death, and Being are as one,
It is a circle. There is no
    beginning and no end.
For that which is the beginning
    is the end of the other.
And that which is the end
    is the beginning of the other.
Surely the lessons of life are
    the wisdom of death.
Those that live in the knowledge
    of what the circle truly is
    have peace beyond measure.

AUTHOR UNKNOWN

ON SORROW

Some of you say "Joy is greater than sorrow,"
  and others say, "Sorrow is the greater."
But I say to you,
  they are inseparable . . .
The deeper that sorrow carves into your being
  the more joy you can contain.

KAHLIL GIBRAN
The Prophet

THE TOAST

May you always have art to charm
your days, a sensible hearth
and friends as dependable as gravity.
May the wind and creatures be as music
to your evenings alone and may your dreams
leave you renewed. May you have an Appaloosa
to ride the outline of blue hills, and nothing
that sickens, and no black sticks.

JAMES BERTOLINO

FOR FRIENDS AND FAMILY

I thank you dear friends (family)
for sharing in my life—
the dark hours, the challenges,
the struggles and strife,
the good times, the laughter,
the love and the cheer
through all and all—
I'm blessed you are near.

STEVE MYRVANG

• 5 •

Native American Graces

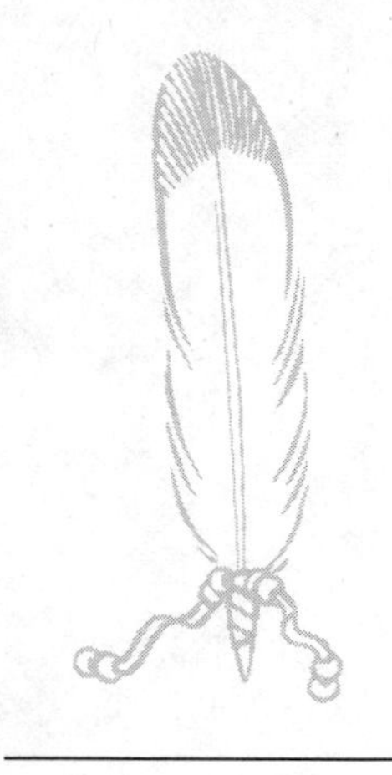

CHIEF SEATTLE

This we know.
The earth does not belong to us,
we belong to the earth.
This we know.
All things are connected
like the blood which unites one family.
All things are connected.

Whatever befalls the earth
befalls the sons and daughters of the earth.
We did not weave the web of life,
We are merely a strand in it.
Whatever we do to the web,
we do to ourselves. . . .

CHIEF SEATTLE

A PRAYER FOR THE WILD THINGS

Oh, Great Spirit, we come to you with
love and gratitude for all living things.
We now pray especially for our relatives
of the wilderness—the four-legged, the
winged, those that live in the waters, and
those that crawl upon the land. Bless
them, that they might continue to live in
freedom and enjoy their right to be wild.
Fill our hearts with tolerance,
appreciation, and respect for all living
things so that we all might live together
in harmony and in peace.

MARCELLUS BEAR HEART WILLIAMS

NATIVE AMERICAN PRAYER
(adapted)

O Great Spirit,
Whose voice I hear in the winds,
And whose breath gives life to all the world,
Hear me! I need your strength and wisdom.

Let Me Walk in Beauty, and make my eyes
ever behold the red and purple sunset.

Make My Hands respect the things you have
made and my ears sharp to hear your voice.

Make Me Wise so that I may understand the
things you have taught my people.

Let Me Learn the Lessons you have hidden in
every leaf and rock.

I Seek Strength, not to be greater than my
brother, but to fight my greatest enemy—
myself.

SIOUX INDIAN SAYING

May the Great Mystery
make sunrise in your heart.

6

Traditional Graces

A BREAKFAST PRAYER
(Thanksgiving)

Father we thank Thee for the night
And for the pleasant morning light
For rest and food and loving care,
And all that makes the day so fair.

Help us to do the things we should
To be to others kind and good,
In all we do, in all we say,
To grow more loving every day.

REBECCA J. WESTON

WE THANK THEE

For health and food,
For love and friends,
For everything
Thy goodness sends,
Father in Heaven,
We thank Thee.

RALPH WALDO EMERSON
(1803–1882)

THANK YOU, GOD, FOR EVERYTHING

Thank you for the world so sweet,
Thank you for the food we eat.
Thank you for the birds that sing,
Thank you, God, for everything.
Amen.

AUTHOR UNKNOWN

GOD IS GREAT

God is great, and God is good,
And we thank Him for our food,
By His hand we all are fed;
Thank you, Lord, for our daily bread.

AUTHOR UNKNOWN

A TRADITIONAL BLESSING

The Lord bless us and keep us, the Lord make his face to shine upon us, and be gracious unto us, the Lord lift up the light of his countenance upon us and give us peace.

(Based on the opening verse of Psalm 67, this blessing has been repeated since at least the seventh century before Christ and has passed into use in the Christian church.)

THE LORD'S PRAYER

Our Father who art in heaven,
Hallowed by Thy name,
Thy kingdom come,
Thy will be done,
On earth, as it is in heaven.
Give us this day
Our daily bread,
And forgive us our trespasses,
As we forgive those who trespass against us.
And lead us not into temptation,
But deliver us from evil;
For thine is the kingdom,
And the power,
And the glory,
Forever and ever,
Amen.

(This great prayer is part of the religious service for all Christianity. It is the model of all prayers for all time. Untold millions turn to this prayer when seeking help, guidance, healing, or solace in every conceivable situation. It is considered the best loved of all Christian prayers.)

THE 23RD PSALM

The Lord is my shepherd; I shall not want.

He maketh me to lie down in green pastures: he leadeth me beside the still waters.

He restoreth my soul: he leadeth me in the paths of righteousness for his name's sake.

Yea, though I walk through the valley of the shadow of death, I will fear no evil: for thou art with me; thy rod and thy staff they comfort me.

Thou preparest a table before me in the presence of mine enemies: thou anointest my head with oil, my cup runneth over.

Surely goodness and mercy shall follow me all the days of my life: and I will dwell in the house of the Lord for ever.

THE HOLY BIBLE, KING JAMES VERSION

7

For Children

A CHILD'S GRACE

Bless this meal, O God, we pray,
And bless us, too, throughout the day.
Keep us safe and close to you,
And kind in all we say and do.

THERESA MARY GRASS

A BREAKFAST GRACE

I thank You, God,
  for this good day.
With time for work,
  and time for play.
I thank You for
  the morning light
And all that makes
  the world so bright.

Help me to live
  this lovely day
In such a kind and
  friendly way,
You will be glad
  that I am here
To help You fill
  this world with cheer.

FRANCES MCKINNON MORTON

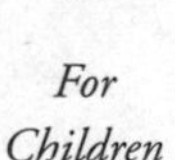

BLESS WITH TENDERNESS

Dear Father, hear and bless
    Thy beasts and singing birds;
And guard with tenderness
    Small things that have no words.

AUTHOR UNKNOWN

THANK YOU FOR THE SUN
(Prayer)

Thank you for the sun,
    the sky,
for all the things that like to fly,
    the shining rain that turns grass green,
    the earth we know—
    the world unseen—
for stars and night, and once again
    the every morning sun. Amen.

MYRA COHN LIVINGSTON

PRAYER FROM ENGLAND

For rosy apples, juicy plums,
And yellow pears so sweet,
For hips and haws on bush and hedge,
And flowers at our feet,
For ears of corn all ripe and dry,
And colored leaves on trees,
We thank you, Heavenly Father God,
For such good gifts as these.

AUTHOR UNKNOWN

OUR THANKS

We thank Thee, Lord, for happy hearts,
For rain and sunny weather.
We thank Thee, Lord, for this our food,
And that we are together.

EMILIE FENDALL JOHNSON

ALL THINGS BRIGHT AND BEAUTIFUL

All things bright and beautiful,
All creatures, great and small,
All things wise and wonderful,
The Lord God made them all.

Each little flower that opens,
Each little bird that sings,
He made their glowing colors,
He made their tiny wings.

The tall trees in the greenwood,
The meadows where we play,
The rushes by the water
We gather every day—

He gave us eyes to see them,
And lips that we might tell
How great is God Almighty,
Who has made all things well.

CECIL FRANCIS ALEXANDER

A CHILD'S PRAYER

O heavenly Father, protect and bless all things that have breath: guard them from all evil and let them sleep in peace.

ALBERT SCHWEITZER
(WHEN A CHILD)

(Schweitzer writes: "As far back as I can remember I was saddened by the amount of misery I saw in the world around me. One thing that especially saddened me was that unfortunate animals had to suffer so much pain and misery. It was quite incomprehensible to me why in my evening prayers I should pray for human beings only. So when my mother had prayed with me and kissed me good night, I used to add silently [the above] prayer that I had composed myself for all living creatures.")

GOD'S IN HIS HEAVEN

The lark's on the wing;
The snail's on the thorn:
God's in His Heaven—
All's right with the world!

ROBERT BROWNING
(1812–1889)

8

For the Earth

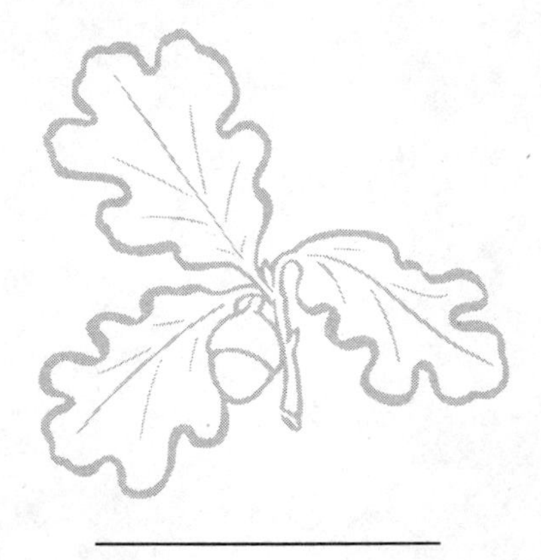

INUIT SONG

And yet, there is only
One great thing,
The only thing:
To live to see in huts and on journeys
The great day that dawns
And the light that fills the world.

AUTHOR UNKNOWN

PRAYER BASED ON PSALM 19

The forest sings God's praises—
the long exhalation of the earth waking from winter
sings God's praises,
and the mosses hear, and the trees,
the trees with their miraculous white leaves,
like angel wings—they hear,
and add their voices
and the pines whisper it,
and the trailing arbutus carries it over the ground
so that all the forest knows,
singing in silence,
who made them in love and joy,
and they stretch to reach Him,
and I feel their singing
    in my hands as I touch them;
    in my eyes as I see them;
    in my feet as I walk among them.
O God, help me to keep listening.

BONITA FOGG SMITH

CALL OF THE WILD

The call of the wild is a restless voice
Of wind and sky and sea;
Beckons all—both great and small
With the yearning to be free.

It drives snow geese in autumn skies
And answers the coyote's cry;
Blows in the mist of mountain crests
And lifts the eagle high.

The thunder of the river's plunge,
The whisper of the desert's dune;
Nature sings a thousand songs
To her jeweled and mystic tune.

The call of the wild is a will within
To venture where few have trod,
With a captive sound that makes hearts pound—
It must be the voice of God.

C. DAVID HAY

GOD'S HANDIWORK

Each time I see a rainbow
Or a nearby turtledove,
It serves as a memento
of God's eternal love.

I feel His presence near me
On a quiet starlit night,
When the moon soars high above me
And gives off its magic light.

A garden filled with flowers,
Caressed by morning dew,
Reminds me of His handiwork
And gives me strength anew.

A household filled with laughter,
A child at mother's breast,
In times of strife, a Friend for life,
By these we all are blessed.

MARY A. SUMMERLINE

TEACH US

Beloved Divine Mother,
Who has become our earth, our skies,
Our waters, our trees,
Our animal sisters, our human brothers,
Our human mothers, our families,
Nurture us always
And cradle us in Thy never ending Love.
Teach us to see Thy Beauty,
Teach us to feel Thy Beauty,
Teach us to *be* Thy Beauty
Wherever we go.

WAVE CARBERRY

GARDEN CREDO

I believe in Gaia the Mother All-tender,
Earth Spirit, maker of gardens,
and in her sons and daughters,
the trees and plants of four seasons.
I believe in the white lilies
and red ranunculus of summer,
and in their seeds.
I believe in the pears and apples of autumn,
the pumpkins, the blue-gray squashes
that nourish our bodies with their meat,
our spirits with their beauty.
I believe in the holly of winter
whose needling leaves and red berries
unite the green of Gaia to the blood of Christ.
I believe in the crocus and tulips of spring
whose petals open like sacred chalices
from which all may drink the joy of the garden.

THELMA J. PALMER

THE REFUGE OF THE GLEN

When I am weary deep within
I seek the refuge of the glen,
My favorite place in early spring,
Where bluebirds nest and warblers sing.

I feel that God is there with me
In every flower, in every tree;
In grassy meadow and rocky nook,
In distant hills and babbling brook.

In summertime I sit for hours
While shaded by the roses' bowers,
And watch a sparrow on a limb,
His song more beautiful than any hymn.

Then on a crisp October morn
The forest Nature will adorn,
With brilliant colors that surpass
The stains of a cathedral's glass.

I search for fruits from vines and trees
As I walk among the falling leaves.
I watch an eagle as he glides,
And think what wonders God provides.

In wintertime when limbs are bare
I find things of which I was not aware;
The nests of birds and squirrels and bees,
And mistletoe clinging to the trees.

But when a blanket of snow is supplied
The world seems somehow purified.
Oh how close to Heaven can I be
With all this beauty surrounding me!

MARY A. SUMMERLINE

TREES!

Our Father, we thank Thee for Trees! We thank Thee for the trees of our childhood in whose shade we played and read and dreamed; for the trees of our schooldays, the trees along the paths where friendship walked. We thank Thee for special trees which will always stand large in our memory because for some reason of our own they became our trees. We thank Thee for the great stretches of trees which make the forests. May we always stand humbly before Thy trees and draw strength from them as they, in their turn, draw sustenance from Thy bounties of earth and sun and air.

MARGUERITTE HARMON BRO

(Margueritte Harmon Bro was an educational missionary in China from 1919 to 1925 and later was editor of *Social Action.* She is the author of some twenty-five books on religious subjects.)

THANKS TO THE SUN

Dear old Goldenface
we praise you
for your beaming light
for the smile of your early rises
for your laughter over the noon
for your goodnight grin

Be sure to come back tomorrow

JAMES BROUGHTON

• 9 •

Musical Graces

His Sheep Am I

Orien Johnson © 1956

HIS SHEEP AM I

In God's green pastures feeding,
    by His cool waters lie;
Soft, in the evening walk my Lord and I.
All the sheep of His pastures
    fare so wondrously fine,
His sheep am I.

Waters cool,
    In the valley,
Pastures green,
    On the mountain,
In the evening walk my
        Lord and I.
    In the evening walk my Lord and I.

Dark the night,
    In the valley,
Rough the way,
    On the mountain,
Step by Step . . . my Lord and I.
    Step by step my Lord and I.

ORIEN JOHNSON

Morning Has Broken

Gaelic melody

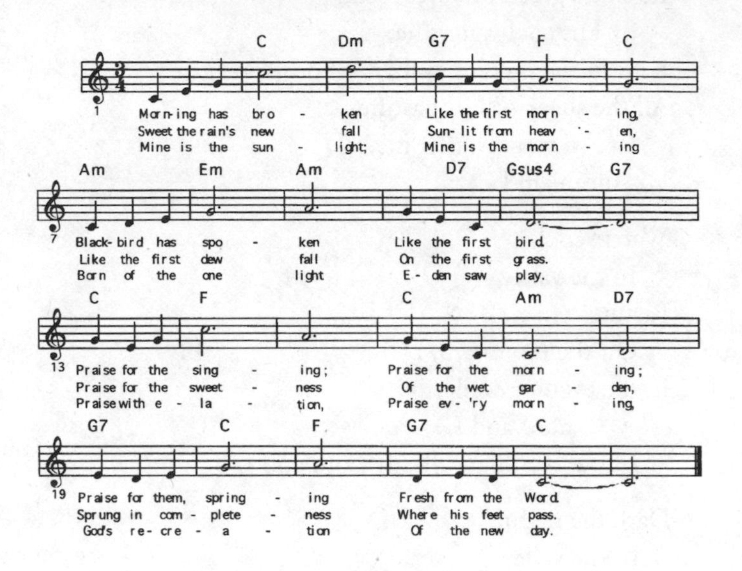

MORNING HAS BROKEN

Morning has broken like the first morning,
Blackbird has spoken like the first bird.
Praise for the singing! Praise for the morning!
Praise for them springing fresh from the Word!

Sweet the rain's new fall sunlit from heaven,
Like the first dewfall on the first grass.
Praise for the sweetness of the wet garden,
Sprung in completeness where His feet pass.

Mine is the sunlight! Mine is the morning!
Born of the one light Eden saw play.
Praise with elation, praise every morning,
God's recreation of the new day!

ELEANOR FARJEAN

Canticle of Brother Sun

Saint Francis of Assisi adapted by Paul Winter

Music by Jim Scott © 1982

CANTICLE OF BROTHER SUN

All praise be yours, through Brother Sun.
All praise be yours, through Sister Moon.
By Mother Earth, the Spirit be Praised.
By Brother Mountain, Sister Sea
Through Brother Wind and Brother Air
Through Sister Water, Brother Fire
The Stars above give thanks to thee,
All praise to those who live in Peace.

SAINT FRANCIS OF ASSISI, ADAPTED BY PAUL WINTER
(FROM MISSA GAIA/EARTH MASS)

Scottish Grace

Robert Burns

SCOTTISH GRACE

Some ha'e meat and can-na eat,
And some ha'e none that want it;
But we ha'e meat and we can eat,
And so the Lord be thank-et.

ROBERT BURNS

Doxology

Thomas Ken, 1637-1711

Genevan Psalter, 1551

DOXOLOGY

Praise God from whom all blessings flow;
Praise Him, all creatures here below;
Praise Him above ye heavenly host:
Praise Father, Son, and Holy Ghost!

THOMAS KEN
(1637–1711)

Mystery

Jeremy Geffen ©1982

MYSTERY

It lives in the seed of a tree as it grows.
You can hear it if you listen to the wind as it blows.
It's there, in the river, as it flows into the sea.
It's the sound in the soul of a man becoming free.

And it lives in the laughter of children at play.
And in the blazing sun that gives light to the day.
It moves the planets and the stars in the sky.
It's been the mover of mountains since the beginning of time.

(refrain)
Oh Mystery you are alive, I feel you all around.
You are the fire in my heart, you are the holy sound.
You are all of life, and it is to you that I sing.
Oh grant that I may feel you, always in everything.

And it lives in the waves as they crash upon the beach.
I see it in the Gods that men have tried to reach.
I feel it in the love that I know we need so much.
And I know it in your smile, my love, when our hearts do touch.

But when I listen deep inside I feel you best of all.
Like a moon that's glowing white, and I listen to your call.
And I know that you will guide me, I feel you like the tide.
Rushing through the ocean of my heart that's open wide.

(refrain)

JEREMY GEFFEN

'Tis a Gift to Be Simple

Words: Joseph Bracket, 18th Century

Music: Shaker Hymntune

'TIS A GIFT TO BE SIMPLE

'Tis a gift to be simple,
'Tis a gift to be free,
'Tis a gift to come down
  where we ought to be,
And when we find ourselves
  in the place just right,
'Twill be in the valley
  of love and delight.

SHAKER HYMNTUNE

Turn! Turn! Turn!

(To Everything There Is A Season)

TURN! TURN! TURN!
(To Everything There Is a Season)

To ev'rything (turn, turn, turn)
there is a season (turn, turn, turn)
and a time for ev'ry purpose under heaven.
A time to be born, a time to die;
a time to plant, a time to reap;
a time to kill, a time to heal;
a time to laugh, a time to weep.
To ev'rything (turn, turn, turn)
there is a season (turn, turn, turn)
and a time for ev'ry purpose under heaven.

A time to build up, a time to break down;
a time to dance, a time to mourn;
a time to cast away stones; a time to gather stones
together;
To ev'rything (turn, turn, turn)
there is a season (turn, turn, turn)
and a time for ev'ry purpose under heaven.

A time of love, a time of hate;
a time of war, a time of peace;
a time you may embrace, a time to refrain from
embracing.

To ev'rything (turn, turn, turn)
there is a season (turn, turn, turn)
and a time for ev'ry purpose under heaven.

A time to gain, a time to lose;
a time to rend, a time to sew;
a time to love, a time to hate;
a time for peace, I swear it's not too late.
To ev'rything (turn, turn, turn)
there is a season (turn, turn, turn)
and a time for ev'ry purpose under heaven.

WORDS FROM ECCLESIASTES 3:1–8; ADAPTATION BY PETE SEEGER (SUNG BY THE BYRDS)

10

Short Graces

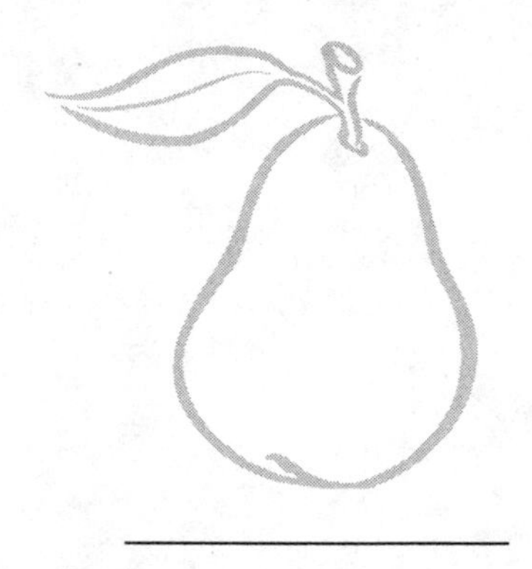

LIVE EACH DAY
(adapted)

Help us to live each day as if it were the last. Show the love we feel for everyone we pass. Amen.

KEN KEYES, JR.

BLESS OUR HEARTS

Bless our hearts
to hear in the
breaking of bread
the song of the universe.

FATHER JOHN B. GIULIANI
THE BENEDICTINE GRANGE
WEST REDDING, CONNECTICUT

EARTH AND SKY

Help us to keep our ears to the earth and our eyes in the stars. Amen.

STEVE MYRVANG

WITH A WINEGLASS (A GRACE)

Male & Female
in one expanding body,
nothing else is like us:
We All Are.

BILL COSTLEY

LIFT THE VEIL

Heavenly Father and Mother,
Lift the veil
That separates us
From the knowledge
Of your love.

May we be warmed
By the glow of Your Divine Love
And freely give to others
The love You freely give to us.

JO-ANNE ROWLEY

ALWAYS WITH YOU

Never above you
Never below you
But always with you.

RUTH ROSE

WITHIN US

What lies behind us and what lies before us are tiny matters compared to what lies within us.

RALPH WALDO EMERSON
(1803–1882)

LIVING SLOWLY

God help us to live slowly:
To move simply:
To look softly:
To allow emptiness:
To let the heart create for us.
Amen.

MICHAEL LEUNIG

I BELIEVE

I believe a leaf of grass
is no less than the journey-work
of the stars.

WALT WHITMAN
(1819–1892)

ETERNITY

To see a World in a Grain of Sand
And a Heaven in a Wild Flower,
Hold Infinity in the palm of your hand
And Eternity in an hour.

WILLIAM BLAKE
(1757–1827)

HEARTFELT

The best and most beautiful things in the world cannot be seen or even touched. They must be felt with the heart.

HELEN KELLER
(1880–1968)

REMEMBERING OUR GIFT

We remember now to thank our Creator
  for all that we are
    and all that we have.

May our sharing with one another
  embody the generosity made possible for us
    by the Giver of the original gift.

PHILIP FOUBERT

YOUR GIFT

Make of yourself a light.

BUDDHA
(HIS LAST WORDS TO HIS FOLLOWERS)

• II •

From Around the World

ENGLISH PRAYER

Give me a good digestion, Lord,
and also something to digest;
Give me a healthy body, Lord,
and sense to keep it at its best;
Give me a healthy mind, good Lord,
to keep the good and pure in sight,
Which, seeing sin, is not appalled,
But finds a way to set it right.

Give me a mind that is not bound,
that does not whimper, whine, or sigh.
Don't let me worry overmuch
about the fussy thing called I.
Give me a sense of humor, Lord;
Give me the grace to see a joke,
To get some happiness from life
and pass it on to other folk.

(This ancient prayer, which turns up everywhere, including the wall of England's Chester Cathedral, has been attributed to Thomas H. B. Webb.)

GERMAN PRAYER

We thank Thee, Heavenly Father,
    For all things bright and good;
The seedtime and the harvest,
    Our life, our health, our food.

FROM THE GERMAN OF MATTHIAS CLAUDIUS
(1740–1815)

AN IRISH BLESSING

May there always be work for your hands to do
May your purse always hold a coin or two
May the sun always shine upon your window pane
May a rainbow be certain to follow each rain
May the hand of a friend always be near to you and
May God fill your heart with gladness to cheer you.

AUTHOR UNKNOWN

THE SAINT FRANCIS PRAYER

Lord, make me a channel of thy peace—that where there is hatred, I may bring love—that where there is wrong, I may bring the spirit of forgiveness—that where there is discord, I may bring harmony—that where there is error, I may bring truth—that where there is doubt, I may bring faith—that where there is despair, I may bring hope—that where there are shadows, I may bring light—that where there is sadness, I may bring joy. Lord, grant that I may seek rather to comfort than to be comforted—to understand, than to be understood—to love, than to be loved. For it is by self-forgetting that one finds. It is by forgiving that one is forgiven. It is by dying that one awakens to Eternal Life. Amen.

SAINT FRANCIS OF ASSISI
(1182–1226)

PRAYER FROM THE NETHERLANDS

O God, who makes a thousand flowers to blow,
Who makes both grains and fruits to grow,
Hear our prayer:
Bless this food
And bring us peace.
Amen.

AUTHOR UNKNOWN

JAPANESE PRAYER

Creator of the world
Help us love one another,
Help us care for each other
As sister or brother,
That friendship may grow
From nation to nation.
Bring peace to our world
O Lord of Creation.

AUTHOR UNKNOWN

ANCIENT CHINESE PRAYER

Heaven is my father and earth my mother and even such a small creature as I finds an intimate place in its midst. That which extends throughout the universe, I regard as my body and that which directs the universe, I regard as my nature. All people are my brothers and sisters and all things are my companion.

CHANG TSAI
(ELEVENTH CENTURY)

• 12 •

For Peace and Justice

TOLERANCE

O Lord, help me not to despise or oppose
what I do not understand.

WILLIAM PENN
(1644–1718)

(Expelled from Oxford University and imprisoned several times for his Quaker faith, Penn was a passionate defender of religious freedom. He founded the state of Pennsylvania, a refuge for persecuted Quakers and a "holy experiment" in religious community.)

A PEACE PRAYER

A golden light is in our midst.
It burns as peace, as hope, as love, as God.
Feel its healing presence pass through you.
Send it to another with a kind and loving thought.
Know this: As it heals the inside,
so can it heal the outside—
for the world is but a reflection
of what lies within.

STEVE MYRVANG

SONNET TO FREEDOM: A WORLD'S PRAYER

The beams that brightly shine from freedom's light
Are sometimes difficult to see.
Still, destiny invites us to unite
Within a proud republic that is free.
When we behold a glimpse of freedom's face,
Its gleaming smile enables us to cope;
For then we have the courage to embrace
The promise of the future with our hope.

Continuing oppression still explains
Why freedom is a necessary goal:
It shatters all the shackles and the chains
Imprisoning the heart of every soul.
  Dear God—in heaven's pale—to you, we pray
  that freedom's light will shine for us today.

ALAN FRAME

FINAL PRAYER FOR NEW GENESIS (adapted)

Dear God, I do not know who You are, but I am in exultant joy before the magnificence of Your creation.

I do not know why You gave me life, but I thank You with every fiber of my heart for having lit up in me the divine spark of light in the vast, incomprehensible universe.

I know that I come from You, that I am part of You, that I will return to You, and that there will be no end to my rebirth in the eternal stream of Your splendid creation.

I do not know why You created light and darkness, happiness and despair, good and evil, love and hatred, creation and destruction, matter and void, and allowed us to choose constantly between the two, but I know that it is my duty and joy to throw down my gauntlet for light, brightness, compassion, goodness, happiness, truthfulness, life, beauty and love.

I cannot define You, I cannot see You, I cannot perceive You, I cannot understand You, I cannot embrace You, but I can most definitely feel You, love You and know that You are.

Please, God, allow us to become at long last a warless, weaponless, hungerless, horrorless, just, kind, truthful, thankful, loving and happy planet.

Help me to show through my life that this is the Planet of God. Please. Amen.

ROBERT MULLER

13

For Contemplation

GOD'S LOVE

If you seek peace,
 you will have none.
If you seek life,
 you will lose it.
If you seek wealth,
 you will find poverty of soul.
If you seek adventure,
 you will be unfulfilled.
If you seek joy,
 you will ache with sorrow.
If you seek love,
 you will despair in loneliness.
If you seek God,
 you will find God.
You will have peace
 that surpasses understanding,
 gain eternal life,
 find true wealth,
 be fulfilled,
 worship in joy,
 and revel in God's love.

SUSAN GERRISH

FOR THOSE WHO LIVE ALONE

(Banquet Feast)

My table, Lord, is small
And my voice seems smaller still.
But I know that when I pray to you
You come and sit by me.

So, please, Lord, join me now
As I pray for those alone.
May they know that you would love
An invitation to their home.

LESLIE BETZING

SLOW ME DOWN, LORD!

Slow me down, Lord!
Ease the pounding of my heart
By the quieting of my mind.
Steady my harried pace
With a vision of the eternal reach of time.
Give me,
Amidst the confusions of my day,
The calmness of the everlasting hills.
Break the tensions of my nerves
With the soothing music of the singing streams
That live in my memory.
Help me to know
The magical power of sleep.
Teach me the art
Of taking minute vacations of slowing down
to look at a flower;
to chat with an old friend or make a new one;
to pat a stray dog;
to watch a spider build a web;
to smile at a child;
or to read a few lines from a good book.
Remind me each day
That the race is not always to the swift;
That there is more to life than increasing its speed.

Let me look upward
Into the branches of the towering oak
And know that it grew great and strong
Because it grew slowly and well.
Slow me down, Lord,
And inspire me to send my roots deep
Into the soil of life's enduring values
That I may grow toward the stars
Of my greater destiny.

WILFERD A. PETERSON

IT WAS SAID WITH SUCH AUTHORITY

I'll give you the gist of
  what was said

It was about love
  and the sayer
said it had nothing to do
  with receiving

He said
  love was all about giving
plain and simple

You could tell this guy
  walked the talk

He made it clear
  you must love yourself
before you can
  begin to love another

The guy reminded me
  of that lover from Galilee

GARY E. MCCORMICK

THIS IS LIFE

In conclusion, I would leave you with this; my first poem:

The mist rising above the crest of a wave
a million selves reflecting upon each other
lasting but a moment, before continuing
This is life evolving out of the depths
of eternity
to color a moment
before continuing.

RICK DUNCAN

THIS IS IT

This is It
and I am It
and You are It
and so is That
and He is It
and She is It
and It is It
and That is That.

O It is This
and It is Thus
and It is Them
and It is Us
and It is Now
and here It is
and here We are
so This Is It.

JAMES BROUGHTON

PERMISSIONS AND ACKNOWLEDGMENTS

Grateful acknowledgment is made to the authors and publishers for the use of the following material. Every effort has been made to contact original sources. If notified, the publishers will be pleased to rectify any omission in future editions.

"'Tis a Gift to Be Simple," reprinted from *Love, Love, Love/'Tis a Gift to Be Simple,* copyright © 1971 by Augsburg Publishing House. Used by permission of Augsburg Fortress.

James Bertolino for "A Spring Crocus: For the Children of AIDS," "A Wedding Toast," "Mountain Lullaby," and "The Toast."

Leslie Betzing for "For Those Who Live Alone (Banquet Feast)."

The Reverend Bob Biddick for "A Group Grace."

James Broughton for "Thanks to the Sun" and "This Is It."

Joseph L. Byron for "Chanukah Message."

Wave Carberry for "Teach Us."

CollinsDove for "Summer" and "Living Slowly," from *The Prayer Tree.* Copyright © 1991 by Michael Leunig. Used by permission of CollinsDove, Melbourne, Australia.

Bill Costley for "With a Wineglass (A Grace)."

Joyce Blakney Duerr for "A New Year" and "Spring."

Rick Duncan for "This Is Life."

Kris Ediger for "I Wonder If God Has a Birthday" and "Thanksgiving Day Prayer."

Thomas Elwood for "Birthdays" and "Grace at Breakfast."

Sheila Constance Forsyth for "Litany for Light."

Philip Foubert for "Remembering Our Gift."

Alan Frame for "Sonnet to Freedom: A World's Prayer."

Jeremy Geffen for the words and music to "Mystery." (The song was created in 1978 on a beach in Key West, Florida. It later became the Communion Hymn for Missa Gaia, a mass in celebration of Mother Earth, performed by the Paul Winter Consort. Missa Gaia is available through Living Music Records, Inc., Box 72, Litchfield, Connecticut 06759. Jeremy Geffen is a medical oncologist practicing in Vero Beach, Florida.)

Susan Gerrish for "God's Love."

"On Sorrow," from *The Prophet* by Kahlil Gibran. Copyright © 1923 by Kahlil Gibran and renewed © 1951 by Administrators C.T.A. of Kahlil Gibran Estate and Mary G. Gibran. Reprinted by permission of Alfred A. Knopf, Inc.

Father John B. Giuliani for "Bless Our Hearts."

Katie Goode for "The 23rd Psalm Revisited."

Theresa Mary Grass for "A Child's Grace," "Blessing," and "Celebration."

Shirley Asano Guldimann for "Easter Invocation."

Eleanor Farjean for "Morning Has Broken." Copyright © 1957 by Eleanor Farjean. Reprinted by permission of Harold Ober Associates, Inc.

HarperCollins Publishers, Inc., for "Blessed Be," from *The Spiral Dance* by Starhawk, copyright © 1979 by Miriam Simos; and "Sanskrit Salutation to the Dawn," from *Earth Prayers,* copyright © 1991 by Elizabeth Roberts and Elias Amidon. Reprinted by permission of HarperCollins Publishers, Inc.

C. David Hay for "Call of the Wild" and "For Father's Day (Little Man)."

Hazelden Foundation for "Our Purpose In Life" excerpt from *Green Spirituality* by Veronica Ray. Copyright © 1992 by Hazelden Foundation. Reprinted by permission.

Alicia Hokanson for "The Island, This Season."

Margaret Anne Huffman for "Advent," "Christmas Eve Dinner," "Easter Meal Grace," "Grace for Dieting," "Grandparents' Day," "Halloween Grace," "Memorial Day Picnic Grace," "Milestone Birthday Grace," "New Baby," "Wedding Anniversary Grace," and "Wedding Rehearsal Dinner Grace."

Thomas K. Hyland, Jr., for "A Hylander's Blessing" and "For Mother's Day."

Ken Keyes, Jr., for "Live Each Day."

Helen Latham for "For a Family Reunion" and "Thanksgiving Blessings."

Myra Cohn Livingston for "Thank You for the Sun (Prayer)" from *The Moon and a Star and Other Poems* by Myra Cohn Livingston. Copyright © 1965 by Myra Cohn Livingston. Reprinted by permission of Marian Reiner for the author.

Gary E. McCormick for "It Was Said with Such Authority," "Lilacs," and "Winter Vision."

Melody Trails, Inc., for "Turn! Turn! Turn! (To Everything There Is a Season)." Words from the Book of Ecclesiastes. Adaptation and music by Pete Seeger. TRO © copyright 1962, renewed. Melody Trails, Inc., New York. Used by permission.

Monica Miller for "I Thank Thee."

Steve Myrvang for "Earth and Sky," "For Friends and Family," "For Our Children," "A Peace Prayer," and "We Close Our Eyes."

Thelma J. Palmer for "A Summer Grace," "December Blessing," and "Garden Credo."

Wilferd A. Peterson for "Slow Me Down, Lord!"

Marjorie Gail Pevner for "Chanukah Lights."

Ruth Rose for "Always with You."

Daniel Roselle for "Credo at Christmas" and "Thanksgiving Grace."

Jo-Anne Rowley for "Lift the Veil."

Bonita Fogg Smith for "Prayer Based on Psalm 19."

Mildred M. Smith for "A New Year's Eve Prayer."

Joan Stephen for "Morning Grace" and "Psalm of Praise."

Mary A. Summerline for "God's Handiwork" and "The Refuge of the Glen."

Thomas Nelson Publishers for "A Breakfast Prayer" by Rebecca J. Weston and "Our Thanks" by Emilie Fendall Johnson. Both poems excerpted from *Table Graces for the Family*, copyright © 1964. Reprinted by permission of Thomas Nelson Publishers.

Jim Scott for music to "Canticle of Brother Sun," copyright © 1982 by Radiance Music, 1430 Williamette #B, Eugene, Oregon 97401. Reprinted with permission. (Words adapted from Saint Francis of Assisi by Paul Winter.)

Joanna M. Weston for "Christmas Come."

"A Prayer for the Wild Things" by Marcellus Bear Heart Williams. Copyright © 1993 by Marcellus Bear Heart Williams. Courtesy of The Greenwich Workshop, Inc., Trumbull, Connecticut 06611.

Norma Woodbridge for "Christmas Prayer," "Easter Song," and "Prayer for Our Home."

Word Music for "His Sheep Am I." Copyright © 1956 by Orien Johnson. Assigned to Sacred Songs, a division of Word, Inc. All rights reserved. Used by permission.

World Happiness and Cooperation for "Final Prayer for New Genesis" by Robert Muller. Excerpted from *New Genesis, Shaping a Global Civilization,* copyright © 1982. Reprinted by permission of World Happiness and Cooperation, P.O. Box 1153, Anacortes, Washington 98221.